TO SEE THE EARTH
BEFORE THE END OF THE WORLD

WESLEYAN POETRY

TO SEE THE EARTH
BEFORE THE END OF THE WORLD

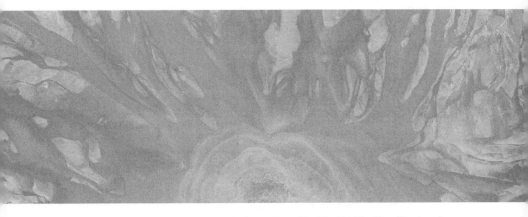

ED ROBERSON

WESLEYAN UNIVERSITY PRESS
MIDDLETOWN,
CONNECTICUT

Wesleyan University Press
Middletown CT 06459
www.wesleyan.edu/wespress
Manufactured in the United States of America
First paperback edition 2017
ISBN for the paperback edition: 978-0-8195-6949-3
Designed and typeset in Minion by Katherine B. Kimball
5   4   3   2   1

The Library of Congress cataloged the hardcover edition as:
Roberson, Ed.
  To see the earth before the end of the world / Ed Roberson.
     p. cm. — (Wesleyan poetry)
  ISBN 978-0-8195-6950-9 (cloth : alk. paper)
  I. Title.
  PS3568.O235T6 2010
  811'.54—dc22   2010027094

NATIONAL
ENDOWMENT
FOR THE ARTS
A great nation
deserves great art.

This project is supported in part by an award
from the National Endowment for the Arts.

CONTENTS

III. CHROMATIC SEQUENCES

PART I   TOPOI

TO SEE THE EARTH BEFORE THE END OF THE WORLD

People are grabbing at the chance to see
the earth before the end of the world,
the world's death piece by piece each longer than we.

Some endings of the world overlap our lived
time, skidding for generations
to the crash scene of species extinction
the five minutes it takes for the plane to fall,
the mile ago it takes to stop the train,
the small bay   to coast the liner into the ground,

the line of title to a nation   until the land dies,
the continent uninhabitable.
That very subtlety of time between

large and small
Media note   *people chasing glaciers*
in retreat up their valleys   and *the speed* . . .

watched ice was speed made invisible,
now—   it's days, and a few feet further away,
a subtle collapse of time between large

and our small human extinction.
If I have a table
at this event, mine bears an ice sculpture.

Of whatever loss it is   it lasts as long as ice
does until it disappears   into its polar white
and melts   and the ground beneath it, into vapor,

into air.   All that once chased us and we
chased to a balance chasing back, tooth for spear,
knife for claw,
               locks us in this grip
      we just now see
                         our own lives taken by
taking them out.   Hunting the bear,
we hunt the glacier with the changes come
         of that choice.

Topoi

1. MORNING

The year and its
   as like as eggs,
     the days

in their crates of season
   we break open
     and the yolk

of fresh sun we scramble
   the runny light into
     a firm

break
   of the night's winter
     helping of the fast.

       *

Yellow dishes—
    forsythia
  set out for the early
     meal of season—

sit the house   yards
    the town
  parks   down together
     to this spring as

to a table
    all set
  in order   just
    So

good to see
　　you and
　　your way found
　　　back.

　　　　*

The arriving coats of smell
　　are hung in the air, butt-smacked and
　　　oiled babies of moment;

and years of taste as touch
　　hug　the senses
　　　to the living;

sweet sour bitter salty
　　some never experienced
　　　again, the gloved fingers

of bananas　so briefly kissed
　　with ripeness; fruit,
　　　grip-shaped thought

brought to the tongue,
　　the finished taste
　　　of words,　an aftertaste

of silence,　the morning
　　glories we haven't tasted
　　　yet

　　　　*

life, as lasting as any one
　　sense, a taste
　　　a sight, an orange mix

of kiss with sweetness
　　for the moment
　　　it exists, finishes and

is swallowed, is also those
   who finish hungry or starve
      to death   which swallows;

the final stage of rattlesnake bite
   is yellow vision,
      light,   then you both go out.

Fear, to the tongue, is metallic: I tasted
   a copper penny   it could have been
      a one-time and final, incomparable

    —How does life taste
   to one condemned
     in that cup   this morning?—

flash of a taste;
   a touch's backbeat, that single shake
     in the whole

coital dance   that whiff of ?

     a one-time and final   taste
            taste   this morning

2. DEEP TIME

Where trees are a sky
   whose spider web
  radio antennas'
      search receives
   the rhythmic static
       of cicadas,

a song arrives
   that died leaving
  seventeen years ago.

       Deep
cumulus leaves—
   whose cloud and Milky Way
  are green,
       and heard but unseen
    insect star births
     have yet to reach us from—

refract the sun
    -light filtered
   through to brilliant spiked
      explosions of nova
    in this hiss

        that one
day our own
    insect sun will make
   in deep time into deepsong.

3. PLANETARIUM

A child already an old man
sits in a rocking chair in the yard
facing into the shadow side
of four elms down the end of the block.

He's heard but hears them for the first time
as the cicadas   he's looking for   just one
bowing its wings with its legs
as he's been told they do   he wants to see.

The sun lowering
on the opposite side of the trees
pierces through   burning open holes in spaces
brilliant prismatic   explosions.

He thinks this is how cicadas' sound
speakers look hooked up to the sky
through the trees   refractive, light show
to the music & this   evening is their show
        the cataclysmic novas   nebulae

4. LUNAR ECLIPSE

You've seen only a planed circle of moon,

the white wafer; the low sky's flat penny

grow into that dime, flipped in the turn

taken by the earth,

      until you see

what's won from behind its veil of brightness

by the lunar eclipse

        a red marble,

a pinball of blood and it's your shot, a ball

of red clay before its pinch into a bowl,

what I want to say and its look

that far away from it.

I want to say it suddenly

turns three dimensional with shadow

shaded in at the drawn

earth-curtain's darkening;

       and that darkness

makes shape-informed light clearer rounding out

midnight,   and moon,

                    once it is that lighted ball,

falls above a night now floored with depth

so dark above you   you can feel the feet

and meter fill with time. New Years confetti each

speck's fall a galaxy ago back into space.

Space back into space restored   beneath the moon

to here in the shading of eclipse.   The distances.

            We have to feel the spatial in what we see

to see clearly   the eye measure in hands and feet;

                       as when we kiss,

distance disappears, our eyes close,

and we see bodily

               in raised detail

a measure deepen into our world

in each other. And what we are

in the shadow the world makes

of our love, by this earth shine, we see

            ourselves whole, see in whole perspective.

5. TOPOI

The plane begins its descent into Newark from the west
at the Delaware Water Gap; the whole width
of the state of New Jersey is the base of a triangle
underlying that approach to its point.

Geography test, problem off the wall
to the ground, whole highway systems
unfold again below, the maps we rode. But at
what point did we become so familiar with

such long perspective we could look down
and recognize the pile of Denver by the drop off
and crumble of the plate up   into the Rockies,
or say   That's Detroit!   by the link of lakes by

Lake St. Clair some thirty-thousand feet
above Lake Erie while just barely spotting Huron
on the horizon?

Some earlier hunter had a similar picture in his head
for getting around, and what he saw seems map
his feet figured   what a Boeing 757
picks up and puts down pacing off

my passing through the world by air.
But we've seen the ground ball up into one
step and stand on nothing else, our footing in
the vacuum, diminished sky of solar space.

Yet we haven't seen again his vision, haven't yet
dreamt from it even such map as he had
hunted by; we haven't seen answered from that garden's
gazing ball whether there is direction after all
the dream-lines

have been hunted to circumference. Like trained bear
dancing on a circus ball, we look down, our feet in a step
from which there is no step off,

this footprint all of step ever taken.
    The hunted step, kept far and fast enough
away from the hunter to keep the distance of its life,
shortens to none between them or is that

shit outcome stepped in, become their one,
in perspective, step from which there is no step out of.
In that sense of   "the surface over which
a phenomenon exists," the earth is the footprint of life.

Gaia's gravity-swayed steps take on orbit,
we in the tropic of balance, in a basket
on her head, a blue wrap of sky, sun
ripens the thin rind of the plane to home.

Sweet fruit of the journey, of all journey,
fruit of all step   home is the sweet fruit
that is all of step that is ever taken.

The earth is all of step ever taken
by most of us, we think; but the aisles of air
we walk about with the seatbelt sign off
hang off our backs   angel's wing or motion

lines such as drawn in cartoons or the tesseract
of four dimensions. Cube sunk in a square of space,
sunk in a space of time. Our cubed world
worn as a helmet among

strung dimensions far distant enough to see
the ball that all our ways are woven from:
sand, the lens grinder's patient hand, sore elbow, head
in the stars, he looks down at his feet. Sunk in time,

the footprint of life is death, the grave
there is no step out of, the compost earth.
The earth is the footprint of life.

6. MANY LOCATIONS

Many locations now are ahead of
humanly possible without conduct
through a technology;
                    we live not yet
caught up with ourselves, the landings offset
by foot pace their space-time for ground transportation.

Unlike stars whose fact is a presumption
of departure or arrival other
than in lived light, we're less than when we are.

We're dated within histories of make
in order to be made whole;
                    we body age
in our times' prosthesis of achievement
as our time;
                    as our years, our state's moment,
a birth condition, enlarges or wastes us,
the long sentenced swing, instantaneous.

7. THE $$-MEN

The bus as technological magic
shoes, the plane, a flying suit not in the style
of tights and cape, more comfortable,
but shared, like the chevron of flying geese
shares in that wake the one at the point makes;
we support our super powers flapping
almost in unison, our money down.

8.

    The instant though, is ours: Euclidean
point without space, taking place as from.

If it were location, anything there
is not the point.—It is
                 position in relation
more to other yet-positions more
                              one
that is everywhere nowhere until pointed
out: we have no point until we have to
                 see say where how far
another is to   or from us
                      continuously
renewed: Call me.
The call made is also in its way

how   point also has to be limited
& in limiting . . . challenged . . .
               What are you doing? . . . . .
always in process; point
               is lived.

9. OLD DEPENDENCY

Sun-like,

a satellite passes overhead
between the least imperious hours
                    of 2 and 5 am.

A signal picked up from Colorado
beams a setting for the time
                    in Chicago back to earth.
My watch sits meditating, on the sill,
faces out the window at tonight's
                    radio sky.

It is built for a connection I am not
that it passes on when I aim at it
                    my time pickup

eye the set I need; and off the knees of its clasp
wristband folded underneath,
                    a timing sun's worshipper—

since I've forgotten how the sunrise set
men's cycles—   listens to its crystal
                    break time down,

its atom tune the seconds . . .   Our body's
band to the watched face of the sun,
                    who tells the wake and sleep,

comes in the style of our skin.   That close
a melanin-melatonin connection. Yet here's an inorganic
                    jewelry

connecting a crystal oscillation through
a radio wave in orbit to
                              setting itself to set my day.

Gemstone cut music on my arm as if
intravenous, cesium vibration, piped
                              aortal

broadcast, drum hour to my heart,
let this renew an old interpretation
                              how we could talk

to rock, listen to plants explain
in the stomach what membranous
                              exchange

is the dawn star with ear of corn;
the watch, its passage, and waking flesh
working to live in time.

10. PROTO-PYRAMID FIGURE

Re-noticing the lines of the furrows
he had plowed   each the same space apart

nearing together on the other side
of the field   he felt the figure

of the eye through   a road drawing away
perspective disappear to not yet seen

those lines of the ground   his bargain
for their food with time   kept uncrossed:

he noticed their opposite   come here
At the end of the day   out of the clouds

The furrowed   light turned over dark   lined up
and came together in the blue

behind a field of sky   he could see across
see the road

of where things come from   the mountain
to the sky they must go up and down

11. WHAT WORD

The fat spoiled cat of fish, the carp, pampered
in the garden pool, surfaces: a bubble
in the level   lines of a purr.

The mirror water vibrates: the mouth's breath,
a spoken surface as thought,   a soundless word
balloon   of concentration   breaks.

The spoken   world rubs against you to own you as,
as the cat does,   one of it.   A placement.
Your smile, your pool of sight touched awake.

                    *

The wakened world's submarines
—our ideologies' spoiled fish—
lift their scale-less indulgences

that our intelligence lays on the tongue
of the silence   of death,   this dragon's breath
freshener of nuclear fire—

And one of these lozenges, we find out
this morning, may lie open at the bottom of the sea
smashed   burst bubble of our technological
meditations;

                and all that is surfacing may be
our leviathan of threat to each other
we recognize—   this caught breath   almost a silent
language among us.

And what has the bubble burst out with
on its breath? The wakened world.
                                    All word
of the living as any longer one of

it is tethered to this brought to the surface,
mouthed breath-clapper in a metal bell,
like the earth's resuscitant bubble of atmosphere,

balling yarn of the planet's one held breath
rolled 'round in as spoiling a lap of orbit
as any swaddled garden pool wove of our
meditations and sun-like surfacing thought.

And the burst bubble of *that* concentration?—
What is the open   it touches against   us?
What claim   of we as one of   do the dead
bring up   even lifted in a joined arms of states?

                    *

Bast, the feline brush by of that cartouche
of breath is the hope of life sucked back
into the born flesh.
                    word   bubble
breath   break that wakens . . . and we would rise
. . .

All connection to us is made surface
to surface:
                microscopic through into,
telescopic out; matter surfaces
as some tympanic resonance,   word snares
on breath, the touch on press
. . .

The pool of a dead face doesn't stir.
There is no longer even a level
rise or fall   of balance.
The oceans of the time men don't exist
include only a drop that we do
and see
            above them another ocean's spray of stars.

WE LOOK AT THE WORLD TO SEE THE EARTH

We look at the world to see the earth,
at the silver, pedestal-ed globe to see the grounds,
we see what we've done with it, what it has
to do with, we see our face bent to a surface;

but what of the world is seen in looking at the earth
any more than the world's measure of minute to a rock
looking, but seeing gets
a return   begets return   gets returned:
the rivers come back, the salmon

We look upon the world
to see ourselves in the brief moment that we are of the earth
            a small fern in a crevice of the cliff face

to see ourselves
in the brief moment
that we are
of the earth

  to see the earth before the end of the world
                            the world
            is mortality, the earth goes beyond us
            is the ours of cosmos
            is our hour of cosmos

PART II THE WORLD, THEN

ABOUT WHAT'S THIS

That railroad man from the song
where *his head was laid*

'neath the drivin' wheel
'n his body never was found

stood up, or rather, bodiless,
seemed to levitate

with the driving wheel balanced
on the top of his head like a hat, a plate—

    "What's this all about?" I asked.

—or an aureole, a glory.
    "What if we need a new technology for glory?" he said, "—not the old
smoking weeds and blood
sacrifice . . . and hearing voices in them. More sense

than I make."   about what's this
all about. Actually working.

The World, Then

The world then
was made up of the same
pieces that turned
into what we have now,

pieces the same that nowhere took
any of what then
I thought was the world and world to come
that came

about: A now. I don't know what   I thought
that put the wrecks of the past back in effect.
as if in progress   back in service. We think
somewhere between right and understanding

we never supposed there'd be this wrong. About
this.

. . .

Facing up to
the night sky is way off
is a vertigo of falling up
off the face of

not so much the earth's *off* into space as off
any hold that was ourselves together
in what balance lasting   in the stars.
                    See

through the bore column of straight up
to the end   of the stars—
That we could be lost
that deeply that we could lose all of thus far
by this far   our moment here's far

off.

. . .

We see the farther away
the more
distant   as the deeper
into time: backwards up to here   how far come.

but time's direction farther   equal this far
goes through town   its whistle is this minute
crossing   and its wall of boxcar all our view.
That lonesome whistle silence of
                                stars   through here sees this—
how you pull this minute of your sleeve off   inside out
then reach in   the past
pull the future out again, in these two distances, your same
unthinking arm of   the galaxy through time.

                                Undoing or one motion through
The Milky Way folding its complexity? The dark drawer.
It's over our head
But (a small thing) lose your balance,   you fall
into that dark shirt never pulled off   your head.

. . .

A haze you can't see by the sky
bright sunny day has—

only by distance.   See
light apotheosize its pale up horizon.   the zenith's white

depth lit.   But we have on and beyond   our hands
to the   sides   a day narrowing to

the density of point and penciled vanishing
the old "thin air" thickened dark   accumulates aerial perspective.

the view through the atmosphere is trickier on the slant
as it sights through the bend of the earth.

the curve collected layers deepen
the heavens' obscurant nothing of nothing there.

we'll trip over the mirage as easily
a distance   as over something here   in this dark

. . .

He wore his glasses
            as if bags beneath his eyes were
        stuffed with
                    his reflection of the lines
and the shown light
            at just the right angle
        on them in them

                    but the point
        where what is written about
                lies
            where whole heavens fall into
                        question
        in his eyes

. . .

          The wall stores
the heat   the stare
                                at it all day
          of the sun   some people

                                pray to some fresco quality
                    on it   some turn their backs
to lean against
the heat   help
                            /hope that the soreness be drawn
                                out of the physical

          Either way   into that hot pollen of stars
our sun mixes in its
          poultice   a crust that when lifted off
                              dissolves what is the pain of
          for us   us

---

          here   a cross
                    made
          nova   new

. . .

As if all physical display were not that
miracle of intent on that mosaic,
our bone tile at the end of the body's firing

              the glaze crackling long after that-
              ting we take as music.
              the swing low of timetables.

Coltrane can be heard
in the silence at the end
of one recording to say

              help   like that. that take
              of stand to wait for a hand while
              more   hands practicing on something

rather than a guess
(as of buses & trains   stop
at which people also standing look up

              though at   differently a
              mosaic)
an art of it   a mastery
approach
makes it not a wait to be completed   somewhere
                                but rather here
                                already touched up
              in practice
              made   up
                          all over the place

. . .

For all the questions
        answer
                then brings up,

those timed-to-life
        questions do
                get answered,

if through dumb time
        the question runs,
                then out.

Timed-out,
        it's neither
                possible nor done,

not even gone,
        to mourn   not been,
                to miss.

There is a true difference
        between the tried disappointment
                and the non-event.

help

---

                answered with:
        Nothing of that great love
             left but the grab
                  for authority
        as the supreme.
             God as looting,
                  storefront to storefront,   the same as
        door to door

. . .

More than a few seconds after waking
I still could feel my thumb burnt where I'd dreamed
I was so hungry I picked up, like a dime
from a sizzling grill, the meat cooking,
and I wondered how long would I stay burned
without that fire of dream, how would I live?

Teapot Boiling, How to Begin the Day

That a beautiful woman gone to pieces
never finishes her cup from a little
coffee shop somewhere says war

shouldn't be convenient as add water
and stir   but somewhere water
begins to boil

the ticking pop
of the gases faster and faster
the first few shots

explode into full fire   surface turmoil
wails from a simple single teapot—
begins a simple day towards its disasters.

Don't believe the writing on the packaging,
it's more difficult than it says.

. . .

A clay pot arrives at the table,
a fragrance as guest
I knew   was coming

who surprises ahead my nose
none the less.   I know
the one who always made this dish   has left.

. . .

Bidders on our own Hells, conservators
who reassemble shadow copies of shadows,
Han lion-dog guards   next up at Sotheby's—

Hell's Han dogs are as man-made as the gates
they stand outside,   blocking this imperial light
from our world. Clock death on every corner

even if only a small stick driven into the ground
by an explosion, a gnomon.
When the sun isn't shining, there is fire for shadow.

But we are on this company line, we are on
our payroll of   *our* clock.
We make lots of money known as

time to spend   but lessen numbers of lives
to fill with it. Noon without either shade or equinox

. . .

a wall turned in the fever sun
to pulsating metal plate or scales
by the lift and peel of its crackled
mud carapace moved in the heat's

waves   a reptilian breathing total
print of the wall on the wall
a small green lizard   not a painting
but the outdoor screening
    documentary of the street
                        the subject speaks
no louder than lizards speak they
don't speak. they wear *they don't*
speak as a sudden blue throat

balloon. somewhere we get that.
cartoon.   overhead graphic.   joke on us.

. . .

The flies cleaning their multiple eye
glass   squeaky clean to bring into focus
the unsighted   corpses of combatant visions:
a sound that hits the chalked nerve—   bone echoes.

Flies know how clean each vision thinks its view
yet   no one can see out of the pair of them;
none see both summit and valley's start
from stood eye level's post. But they all fall.

Some try   see not so multiple of one's own view
as to regress   insect   be lost humanity facing
opposing mirrors both faces of war   their view
ripped into its infinite regressions—

multiple eye. And that sound—   he cried at
the crossroads the buzz chalked across his middle

. . .

the split in the head of the Janus
figure is the placed overlap
facet we have to see around to look
at the present it is   between the ears.

The past sees back where the disease comes from,
The future sees your life once you survive
Who will tell this present moment   mother
of both   that you are sick, who has the station

to stand outside the blindfold these faces
put on time?   The present can see
that the darkness which can curse this gift's delight
is to act through eyes locked someplace else

and trip over the cure or step into the leper's shoes
not looking down   inside the step   between

. . .

With bushes for thick glasses
we can see who is the wax
of this talking

candle.
Deadheading the spent flames
to encourage a re-bloom

only makes the ashes see light again
as darkness,
feel their way across a blackening floor of faces

until every one is theirs: heaven
a plain of ashes.
We can see

the new flame actually as prevention of the new,
see it against itself,   only an incinerant, not light

But we can see the star we
guided by   stay us wrong
by our failure to see its failing
                hold within us

        a sky even larger than turn.   In that.
the drift of its record   needles the law inside out,
the people into the street,
                and guides that guide us   into the ground.

. . .

A thin line drawn on the morning
as if in sand no one's taking seriously,
the finger drawn through the thin powder
of cloud on the sky,   a plane has marked up
the day already,   the attacks begin.
A new uniform for the figure of dawn

The times to find shade from these zeniths
is what time it is now, a suffering from
shadow to shadow (sun not the graceful
golden fringed umbrella of the honor
that comes from casting none, of giving light
without burning and blindness). This time falls short.

The line falls longer. The gnomon, pointer
of sun, staked in the crown of earth's curve,
falls down its side in rotation; the time bleeds.
A burning bush is afire, ashes, not speech.
in its setting. The one good of its ember,
to see what its fire destroyed before dark.

"There are things that I would otherwise
be bothered by," he said, "—my own death, for example."
I said my life.

"Everyone will die sometime, but when I see
the universe as a whole, it gives me," he said—
I said I can't see.

"—a sense of longevity," he said. "I do not care
so much about myself as I would otherwise . . ."*
The matte oxblood glaze

on a six inch, five century old ceramic piece
bothers me   that I won't know how to
do that and do this because each word is

in a jar with a thickness
of the unseen inside surface out
          across the universe

*Abraham Loeb
from "The Dark Ages of the Universe," *Scientific American*

44

. . .

        Distance works
like a defended border feet away   that waits
for when I can get to it   to shoot
chasing us away   The soldiers are the curve of the earth.

On my back   when I look up   at
the night sky   the stars are fences
just above my nose

       that the earth is sliding under.

spiral galaxies,
those ancient halos,
just as well without our heads
to balance their glories
over

better
our foot on the hi
hat cymbals ringing in the spot
light, golden sizzle of the
drums

under that music

the level

The glassed bubble floated in that fill
of liquid: same in its align to gravity
your ears' balance   floated in your eye level.

The body plumb. Her head, foundation to
the sky bowl overhead   the world in it
(she how t'ings git right-ed   [see below])

---

some people might say dirty   the street was   simply disorderly
it was busy   it had no step   all this busyness could move in
sun come between   the buildings even   barred the way
the smells   stayed 'round their stalls   smoke hung   loosened from
the fires   by hotter afternoon air
simple   disorderly
she cut loose   off   into some dipping danced walk wildly
smooth enough she didn't have to   hold the pan of mango halo
on her head   the whole street   fell into it   bathed in it
balanced again
lak dey hat tek de bush bat o
like they had taken the bush bath

A swaying path swallowed what we gave it
for directions by foot

until we no longer understood
the laciness of our maps

and we sat down in a field of eyelets   *(hope woke open,*
and copied the direction of patterns   *a sowing)*

in the forming dunes   in their written over
their own writing—   or the floating schedule on

the silvery back of the river
snake always new

from its shed moment—   we copied the runoff unending of
its ink.   We drank.   It
made us black   Earth

The red spot on two mating cranes
was their prisoner;

but it was their dancing
that would not let go

of their beauty: the bruise of
who holds who   the half

missing half   or the accomplished egg of
the masked dancer half in the crane suit;

that spot is almost an unoccupied
music   in our time   that won't let go

someone dressed up like nature
trying to dance up a future.

Putting on paint and feathers, stepping one
of us through survival, do we all—

If I teach this phoenix to dance would it
partner my way to walk, tell time, would I fly—

Unable to be anywhere but here
can I get out of here the secret how

to hold my spot between steps
in that burning mid-air to the next—

How much secret of my own step can I get
turned over to me

by the torture of possession in this mask,
this interrogation   of ground going after the air?

To wear the moment costumed in   a feather's present,
its plumage consequence of scale's event nailed on,

spots swimming before its eyes   is to be
possessed by, mated to what mask we've made see

and what it sees   cast in the steps thrown on the ground:
ourselves as messianic bird cult far behind

the celled machines of our disappearance,   sees us
making up wings to save a bird among our species

with sticks and wax
a beg

to be taught a dance back
from over the edge   of the end.

. . .

Stopped against
a current   in midair,

the gulls while lifting rotate
in place,   turn
as though the world
turned for them,   and drift off:

That we could shift direction so
gracefully.

            Is there no backtracking
hypocrisy to flight,
is it possible to lie to
wind?   Ancient

Egyptians at death weighed
life in a balance against the feather
of truth.   That feather,

in truth . . .

. . .

      The lathe that turns the necks
of the winter geese
into that scroll of the heron's

      is the seasons
's turning
that shaves the tone from my whiskers
to gray dust   and clean

      my neck for the guillotine
of my sticking it out
for so long.

. . .

A cloud is
whatever it is
on average
only eleven minutes
the elephant
polar bear   the whole gone.

Lasting
should be counted
whatever measure
fulfills its form,
the word occurs

occurs,
but extinctions
have risen
into a jet stream
screening
the contrails'
global flat-line

across the monitor
blue
cyan view we've always
plotted comings from,
our future

even when
the glass
was black and static
with stars. clouds of
how long

. . .

A lamp's fingers
—not dripped completely
free of light—
smudge the room in
                    -to what
          we see
everything except
behind the chair's back:
the corner's tried to keep straight
face.   its turn away

From cute inchoate fingerpaint
to the schooled illusions of depth

the blurred edge of seeing around
the corners   their round edges that turn

off into out of sight   the ball
round of it all off   into smoke—

my eyes   focus into
the tweezers of vanishing point—

Pull out of that nothing
the splinter's vault of ceiling above daylight

unattributed   unpainted   pure

. . .

Its 93 million miles are one
of those both seconds and
grown   inconceivable in years before
                  we see it born   light

The child spill that spells the shapes of
matter to us, matters and names as sight
the colors   recites its numbers to numinous
itself   even counts before

the light arrives light
like a timeless child   plays with time
like fire. burn.   okay un-burn back.

But consequence is our print and finger paint
and what we do doesn't disappear
from what is done.   We fire, then

wiping the gun clean
though only that other of play, even
if the fingerprint is gloved into
thin air,   the air inside is blood

        the kid's
killed his brother
this is how
day found its twin.

night.   and the night twin its
eclipse.   one black and one blood.

. . .

Inside our moment,
the ceilings we build

put the cap
back on the light container.

    A Michelangelo up to
the roof of his chapel goes

only as far as his nose;
just past its bridge is spilled   light,

its millions of unlit years.   millions of
Christs   deaths old.

    Yet is the crime that hasn't begun
its committing yet   of time or number—

or maybe yet done but not there anymore
before even word to know—

an act not understood as criminality
belief not comprehended as atrocity—

our innocence
in the process of discovering

our ignorance   the triggers of its doings
the guilts of its art   the wound and scar

      of our luminosity

PART III CHROMATIC SEQUENCES

Chromatic Sequences

1

Form in early movies   flickering
leaves   in the outline of the canopy,

color lost as if each
leaf alight were a dart of flame off

green   gone ashen to the eye,
each leaf a page-smoke   the distance

each page has come
to history: the haze of

each past   raises its shade of dust each veil
its valley of living   the distance

between it and the next like tree rings
the steps   as much an aerial

as mortal perspective   The trees bend in sequence,
the eye watches   thin air,   but sees the wind.

i

(*What Color Photographers Call the Magic Hour*)

The colors of light
arrived as a time of day,
sat in the whites only.   *Formal or not*

the torch of film caught up with changes and American
color   photography was invented with blood.
Everything turned golden brown done   in a low sun. The cities burnt.

2

we were not seeing movement
the frames put the leaf
each time in a different place than
we remember seeing it before.
we were not seeing movement,
the frames were slower
than we could ignore
what looked like time were measures

taken: there were no steps except in place
where place was
taken   as happened
          to have got that moment's seat

taken   from there
to here there was no movement between them
we were seeing   it was only seeing we saw
                    making live   what we saw

---

from that viewer/ in that seat/ I never saw
'til now anything up to now until now

that maybe I haven't seen anything
I've seen but the betweens

lined up the moon the hills at the horizon
the stretching fields the riverbank trees

river the road all going different speeds
and at some point between them they even

change and go different directions than
my moving
now and be
fore ground and back when
this is was
beautiful even in between

ii

About the trees bending as a seeing
of the wind:

I use this sighting all the time
but clearly see the wind as no clearer there
in its footsteps   than I see

marble or wingfooted bronzes flying than
the look   of movement

see its alias   the invisible
man filmed   but have
only a crushing of snow afoot

Such passing for nothing
such crushing of surface, mountain quarries into
cities   such crunching of light, the present bent,

lensed into this moment
we see   everything moving out of
sight

3   *(Chromatic Spatiality)*

Recall the car, the eight people cramped inside,
the large landscapes of talk and
excitements often in the wrong
lane   opened by faith and innocence,
both in which we innocently had so little
faith, proceeding through the closing openings
in traffic just in time.
                    Beside the road,
recall someone had set the sapling
of a small bright willow in
the huge space eventually
its grace would take,
and how the color of it that spring
already filled

iii

The spaces of color are more than simple
aerial perspective
                    —those waves layering
away each color to that blue
so barely seen it's clearly some place else—

go in other directions, create
even other separations
                          than heaven and earth.
i.e., the increase of intensity in that
line   of sight towards me
                              the closer to
me if me (=   / *here*
is a color   also depicts location and place
                         here
                         in this country   as used
            to be in its restaurants and restrooms

4   *(1948: Art and Third Grade)*

Closely observed realities gain ground
over religious and classical subjects
The real have a hard-edged horizon near the middle
Not much to balance one at a time   but together

extremely uncertain as resolution   vertiginous
All kinds of smart alignments and blind pairings

Earliest of those purely observed what
I felt only myself see   by the third grade
was meat in the butcher shop   pig's feet
the skins looked like my seat partner's hand

and I felt   this sadness for her   she was ugly and
she wasn't supposed to be being white
it was my secret that I could see it
as meat   and supposed to be s'pose to be really looked at

iv   *(not in the Folkways Collection)*

A single voice

this stray singing,
the vocal line

of an assembled
unthinking   *in the night of prison-farm day,*

from which the eerie anarchy
of it all

derives a solitude.   *see d' blindt-ness step out d' way*
                            weren't nothin' there, but somebody step away
          'n I cud sing all outsite
          m'self

5   *(Darkly)*

Some of them are more of light than
they are a color   the flower's ultraviolet
that in a certain cloudy sunlight blurs
the limiting borders out of sight and glows;

or ice with the sky running around inside
its facets switching the flashlight blue
to milky green almost phosphorescent,
a glow-in-the-dark moment for in daylight.

Glass is always light in that it's not there
as a color   transparency is thin air
until you smack into it clearly   a lie:
everything you saw   on some other side.

Some of the colors tar baby the light
into not getting away from as color,
like the hole that swallows everything
and never shines   and were never color

anyhow to some   only something black.
Like back when Ellington's music was only
nigger noise or, if even music, only popular
not art so clearly on the other side.

Whatever side of light this is of seeing,
this is that "darkly" raised to seeing through
in American glass without distortion
of any kind of wisdom or having seen.

How far off that surface
does it have to bounce before
blue dissolves back from
color into light?

6   (*The Metaphor of Impressionism*)

Rather than the usual projection
into road or path, this daylight retracts
to its step, its spot short of direction;

not mossy still meditation   set in green flooring,
a plain of stones each its own horizon
spilling into the dark cycling between.

The fierce push the spot creates appearing
and disappearing as step   each step taken,
a random blink for footing: day   not stone.

An unrest dabs us on this instant of light,
not balance, not dance; the light's paver forward,
then next day, back; the leap from side to side
the leg rays of the shine puppeted

betraying the star breaking up through the leaves,
the clouds overhead. Like wind, we have no
haloed shadow dappling the ground.

vi

your skin is always in variation
in iridescence even with your own
you don't blend in even if everything
else boringly does you have the accent
you can dress in tune with your color
as something you already have on
a basic black yet your color changes
with the color complement you frame it in

it's the armor the color forces in
defense against the racism it draws
the stiffness of the skin the hardened weight
of nothing there but light and perception
not even the fact of wave length and point
you want everyone's boiling points made
(out) of your skin burned out of your skin,
it's the armor, not the color, you want to remove

7   *(advances in latitude)*

In this latitude the leaves
are more beautiful shot
from their trees.   The object

to secure the movement of
artillery   lines also lines clearly forwarded as
coverage of news.   The art of engraving

records a Civil War sniper   the leaves edited out
taken out in the *leave in/ leave out* of working the metal:
he is drawn hit   through his cover,

a foliage transparent to the picture as
well as to the shooter.

     This picture, the double plate printing,
is an important   page in journalism,
it exposes in the line between

the two,   the limitations
on size for newsplate at that time   and the piece
together of seeing, of what is printing and what is

important   A line
which   would not disappear in the appearance
of photography as newer news, as more

there, nearer
as at   and seamless with   the time
it happens   rather than when crafted. A better story,
     but asks its seeing, were you looking or shooting.

vii

        The still   green latitude
of event within which
the light in happening can commit

not just the sight noun
here   is
        but photography's flip verb to

        shoot
on sight
by which to see.   The action.

Death's instant of grief and date
of publication relate
        each independent of the other

        what are you grieving
there is no universal present
moment   Now it is too late

WHAT THE TREE TOOK, ON THE TABLE

Wood that has grown around
a fence post
over the years enclosing

it   the metal in a swirl of grain
a tree that has taken
a bullet from the civil war

shot suddenly exposed in a tabletop
being made
grown into the open by hand

seats us
at the bench of our own
consequence   shown all around us

we don't get away
we don't get off   race
though we know genetically does not exist

does not erase but is
enacted as our history in us is enacted as
American   the tree

does not ungrow   the shot unfire
the whip unlash from the hand having
to build here   nor its scars unscar   but to remain
        in grain

Drawing on what is there
the crayoned jets coloring within the lines
of the sky   flower and circle simple at

that speed
a kid's   they circle around and show you
what they did

An air show
mostly the diagrams of feeling that
the Fair crowd and wind feathers away as

not real   this isn't the bombing—   war birds
darkening the sky and ground with their map of hits
coloring in   someone other than us's day.

But it is   real   it's just that.
here at this time the real act is
this move: the hands up   shading the eyes to see

the sky more clearly,   is the same
as one made at real fighters coming in.
but without the drop   this   book preparing to run

The same sense
of sought safety from
what is there to see,   then your actions
drawing on what is there

9   *(Question to the Director)*

The film's subtitles say this is camellia
not peach blossoms   that appear in the stream
to flow from between two rocks
at the base of the garden wall   from next door

Were this the original legend in Chinese
where the fisherman traces the petals
back to the crevice which is the entrance
to paradise   the petals would be peach

but this is a Japanese movie
In the samurai movie maybe
battle is met   with the fact of paradise
or at least the threshold response of how it is entered.

These days it's more some rote unexamined reading than just according
to the screenplay: paradise seems instead to trigger the fighting

10 (*Architectural Drawing*)

A dome is the support
                of the bridge-in-all-directions,
            anywhere the weathervane
                        seated on it points.

The arch of each foot
                stands on half the dome   of human balance,
            the start point   of the arc made step   our walking is,
                        a colonnade of landing, uplift, then falling
forward.

                The course the great domes of this program take
            to bridge over mortality   they think
                        is to shape time and history,

or their stomp of progress   ---arcing up andfallingdown,
                the great capitols
            each atop the other's emptied footprint.

Geometries have narrative,
                story,   program the building poses
            in its fit to the senses,
                        the spatial drama of its lines
as built idea.

                Even the heavenly dome's turning up
                    is upside down made begging
            bowl   for wandering oceans
                        for others' souls exploitation;

the capsized human balance hung   an upside down,
                the foot's upturned arches cupped into a ship's
            hold   carrying each step's ground
                        gained by trampling another's.

The one who throws his feet up on the rest
                    is taken over
          an edge the earth shouldn't have
                              for falling off itself—

a deceiver's map—
                    for flattening its curve into collapse
          from cathedral grade
                              line to old scratch.

11   *(Architectural Program)*

The insides
of a space, the human
in a volume,

something
internal like the room
of the Pantheon—

by which the plunge and lean
on the shaft
of light through the oculus

as it is poled through time—
also pulls through Grand Central
as the tall windows' oars

in slant hour
of light   stroke the floor.
The traveler

in this volume,
in this
underway.

xi   (travel structure)

Whether the plan is to cross a river
whether the plan is to fly away
home
                      travel
is a transitional structure
its doors in different places.

That wreck we just passed
is the exit to old Penn Station
long gone
                  a building travels
through time when the present doesn't
 debark its reference   to the original

Had this not been our time's
take off from the base
idea of a door
                      as an entrance to
the city   we could have picked up
our Virgil where that man is standing

on 33rd.   It had been the Baths of Caracalla
here. Before and after
its time, waiting for him. Never having left
its reference   the station.

12

The building is up,
Or the last meeting is   attended to
The surprise of no business,

Or the wings watch the stage
of something straighten its back from
A bow to applause returned

to its own natural posture,
The ground still there, or
The ground is still there not being news again

happens again,
And a next step is fresh without thinking,

Yet the way of finish opens
only as far as that finish, no further.

No vision. You should worry about living here.

13

the list of   if
    you live

what you'll have
    to live with

drops and rolls
    open across the floor

each night
    for tomorrow   shimmering

in the lake   light column
    of moon   the sun's

flaming cloud pillar
    to follow   one

after the other
    across

the water   the listed ripple
    items

move the
    dispassionate line

you are bound to:
    the story

the story cutting deep
    into your flesh

each passage
    another passage

PROFIT FULFILLED

The sun runs
its trade of migrations.
In the one
of tears home to cloud,
some
of the tears   overboard,
a loss,   some
of the thrown to drown,

a time:
daily, which never returns forever,
except to look
at daily things this way.   No return.
The passage always there. This is what came
Of the profit.

---

*

as long as you have is
    as long as you have hold

of it   the thread
    embroiders your palm

with its line of fortune
    and takes as it does so   its wages

its blood

MAN WITH THREE DEGREES

(for Tony Halfhide)

When he opened the door on the passenger side
and it spoke that need-oil croak of a greeting,
he said, "This ain't good, y'know. You ain't got
no ladies keepin' it oiled fa ye . . . ?"
speaking to things in that Trinidadian
straight to it talk when he speaks.
I never have a defense in his no
dressin' it up court. "Y'don' need much."
his mantra: he don't eat the meat,
no dressing on the vegetables.

I've always admired how right he is
all t'while he never say so 'less he's ask . . .
"Truth don' take much word; most of
your time it take seein'.
I work only so I have time not to
work . . . Y'don' need much."
The only thing I ever heard him say
him need—women, cars, alla that, no—
was to look at the ocean.
"I have to be where I can see the ocean."

PART IV PLAYGROUND AND PARKS DEPARTMENT MUSIC

EGG GATHERERS

The Emperor sent his scholars
out into the countryside to collect
the people's songs as they were sung

that what got the morning up on blocks,
the wheels stole   you got to walk out to it,
crawl't up underneath for the cool
to lay the sun   golden yolk
in a iron white-hot sky blisterin'   days
the poor has to sell to pays for less to eat

No beauty in that
Send food instead
send food

we'll sing any damn thing you want

WAR SONG, CHILD'S FLUTE

for Hafez

The flute from the drumstick bone
saved from the grownups' chicken
dinner for his brother come home

that Hafez made in the kitchen
weeks later
                   he can really play.

Bone wind-chimes months older ting
ting in the quiet window bay
only bones holler from and bring

the word inside of who is
coming and who is gone.
A bone's been once inside gives

out onto a landscape of beyond.
There, the flesh can be touched in a sound,
his name, a craft of memory, a song.

THIS YEAR

On the lawn
            only two of
the trees pull on

that sweater of lights
            around bare winter's trunk
which is—   the holidays—

only enough
            for two   gifts
left after the storm.

NOTHING NEW

A hailing violin, its thin arm
raised out of the brawl for the song's help:

there's always a fight after the drinking
and singing, there's always one instrument

that knows our cries for help in some song.
It's animal gut, the hill fiddle off a shelf,

the trumpet's snatch through the bell, the sax's sharp gaff—
their whiskey burnt throat raises the gall.

Music clears out the belly for us and bleeds
the wound clean, we make up with our life.

NEW WORLD ORCHESTRA

The definite number of notes in the symphony
to be played each had a jar, fired clay
but in all different shapes, one for each note,
a condor, a lizard, a monkey, a mouse, a woman
with birds for hair, a man with conch feet;
all were blown over a hole in odd spots
of their design; different patterns
on a fish blew a different tone within the
range of fish notes, and the same applied
to all the animals. One player to every note
made an orchestra. Each song had its particular
orchestra and order of breathing that exhaled
the note each player blew like an answer
to his name in a roll call all going down
the list for each note for each jar.
Most of the soundings together had other jars
as in fish with heron, pig with snakes sorts
of grouping which together made a body
that spoke its voice on internal meaning.
The whole history and literature of the people
of the jars was in their playing.
When the people suddenly disappeared
nobody remembered why all these jars were full
of holes and could carry nothing.

SONG

A communal instrument
with one note per player,
per person, per jar.

Non-utilitarian
shapes and openings
all the music

we can recover
bone and one fingerprint
from 300 fired clay jars.

Each note a jar with this thickness—
a fingerprint from the unseen inside
surface out—   of the touch

of silence. I hear what
stands   around   what
contains each word   my body
                            writes   What
                            what

NEW WORLD ORCHESTRA IN THE MARKET
OF THE WEAVERS

In the market of the weavers
a man wears a poncho of chickens.

He wove their scratchings to a fatness with corn
now they are woven together by their feet

worn over his shoulders to market
they hang upside down,

what they will bring in weight
opens their wings around him as if to free him

A clay figurine of a woman has a row of birds for hair
they lean over her forehead   a trim peck of bangs

except that from their beaks they hang a tapestry of her face
their tails tilt up to fan a headdress   a nimbus above the song

you can play with her
She is an instrument of the wind a clay flute.   Quito,

were we to discover the lost sisters of her orchestra
their song would play away each night notation of stars

into the mouth of a jar until the sky empties
into the loss of their music.

They are girls the three ships
I have seen bathing   in a black mirror, a seeing glass.
They are no good to me

Good has no way home from what goods it brought
They are three ships   there are three holes for the hulls
the mouths of their hold

The stacks of unspoken
decks   of shadow.   Populations
of insides   wind over the lips of their openings.

American Jazz Quartet

1. *piano*

IN THE LOBBY, NOT THE DOORMAN

In the evening when people are returning home
anxious to abandon the strain of these attentions,
he comes downstairs from his apartment
and stakes out the bench in the lobby
by the elevators where he has everybody
who enters the building trapped
into socializing with him, if by even
no more than an annoyed nod and a tired
look away from a cheer come of the predatory.
    Their dresses, how good they look, how he'll be up
for dinner at their place in a minute,
how he knows you out there makin' all that money.
    The people in this building are out there
making like he must have at one time.
Or done, made it and sat down. These floors aren't cheap.
He's harmless. But how we haunt our own success.

2. *bass*

URBAN SPECIFIC

standing on the corner begging
for company   a little change

in conversation   something different
made   of to have to come up with

by the time see you later   or else
be in that killing

loneliness of a room   even on the street
stopping people   still left alone—

old   crime   neither poor nor disorderly
just vagrant time's   old crime of age

unaddressed   victim nor perpetrator   just
a man whose only empty pockets are of people

come around   asks if you can spare a little
while   so he can make the train home

3. *saxophone*

THEN THERE'S THIS ONE, PICK HIM UP

pick him up and take him to the jail
of his winnings, take him into house arrest
up from his success, winner lifted
out of his easy to get to by people, drive

the diamond under his fingernail
up through the flesh to pimple as
his wearing,—poppin' light in folks' eyes—
having his nothing come from

funny money. His is real, nothin' but
but a callous disease from discipline
that cuts him off is no joke

no plus
size chile who's got   nor his own
he's somebody else's crime for his time

4. drums

TITHES FOR CHARITY

An angry generosity
comes from the careless hold he has
on what little he has;
     much is taken.

And angered if not from that, then that
he goes along with his losses too
passively,
     too pride-hustled to question.

     So, he
is always wanting back,
never clear he has given, only sure
the gleaners expect too much.

     Then, angry resentment
at the little he has for spill
compared to the stash his privilege has
to flurry from for him, for white's own
     on its white landfill,

that cold storm of trickle down
from coffers vast and out of reach,
privately owned as the sky,
     the deaf sky.

Summer boats, migrating south down the lake
to dry-dock.   Sky reflects in the puddle;
on the grass, necks raised, geese stage for flight.

Geese boats rowing a sky blue wind reflect
in the lake surface, wavy lined entry.
Autumn leaves turn a page of color.

SIGHT READ ON A COUPLE STARS

(for Sun Ra)

A couple of stars late
                 arriving into place,
but these are the morning's
            traffic helicopters hanging;

the stage lights lit along
                the bottom of the curtain,
the reddening
           Lake Michigan horizon.

The lake's line,   on which
               the baton sun makes its
downbeat for the day,   strikes up
        the water   pillar to the sky.

That shimmering wand opens
              the orchestral world we play in
     on time (or missed cue),   wherever
      we come in, our

jump in/ origin we don't understand
             making/as   anywhere.
     Creation is arrival
       on hit it   make it/ right on

time   Where ever in space it's playing
              song on
    point
       by point, note by

note improvisation   a score star by   star—
            the lights on the cars
     down   Lake Shore Drive
            —of the galaxial journey   star by star

("Ring! . . .")

for Richard Wright

Coin peeks through two opening slots   awake;
the blue ticket printed with cloud pops up.
Change ringing inside,   a singing bird.

Loose change of faces adds up rush hour.
The platform stacks those profiles into rolls
the trains cash in for the large bill,   the city.   (*and the rat!*)

———————————————————————

Anglers fishing for buses
    wait at the stops,
wade into the streets to look
    for something coming.
With none of the fisherman's
    wealth of patience
to float, they snag their hooked
    talk into the news
and tear the world apart;
    in branches of trees
plastic bags motormouth
    on and on about ugly.
A sewage of the morning's
    bad feelings
rises around their feet,
    waters their lotus.

In town, floors of
    cloud and deep water
turn men into fish beneath
    their desk screen's surface
chased by serious bigger.
    Riders turn into reflection,
egret and catch. And which
    is which in this wait out
in the sticks, time standing
    over them?
Hooked into the virtual
    by the real
bus so late, they head back
    home and go in
online. The flower that was
    an idea

blooms among its key pads,
    under which small fish
shelter and come up with air
    they encase—

like a getting aboard for travel—
    their egg ideas in   bubbles,
those carrier balloon
    cartoons above the heads
of people   say,
    in the world of comics.
The present, laughing, lives off its catch
    of the last minute
that makes eggs out of
    a deadline, breakfast of champions.
The anglers cast for this connection.

NINE CHICAGO POEMS

To Reg

1   *season opener*

The ants are licking open the peonies
unwrapping the seal to the tight globes
of bloom   they gang up on
and chase away a ladybug
I can sit here   on the porch stoop
as on the step   of an amphitheater
and watch   ours
is a great sports city the tour
guides say   even the house roofs
are bleachers   some ball is always in the air
ready to open   its colors
fragrance like stadium food
scent reaches the street   our mouths drop
open   tongues about to do the work

2

The wind is so high,
the lake surface contracts
in a gasp

The waves jump straight up.

Our side must be winning.

I can't hear
the crowd of whitecap I see
from the bus run

The joggers and cyclists
look as though hysterically
they carry,

themselves,   the news
and breaking sound   that maybe

There's not another side
to water   nor to the whole of
what we play

We field against a fog,
or, the home game in solids, ice
in a change of uniform

We contend against what is
and is ourselves   though

We want a side that isn't
ours to have of
the universe   to have us on our feet

like the waves cheering on
this morning this morning

We want our messengers
to lie   a pool of good news

dead silent
at our feet for us to walk
open.   Our winnings
winning or not: still won a life

that lets us live it
the excitement   of winged ankles,
seas of dancing streets in the envelope.

3

When the waves jumped straight up, the messenger
Sand smashed them to pieces for winning

When the surface fainted back, the stampeding
Sky sank its foot in that face to leave winning

There were two countless words for the score
You hear the roar of silence over winning

Someone screaming, What are you doing, what are you
Doing   Something answers, I am winning.

Doing nothing is thrown out the window
To eliminate that way to deal with winning

We burned gridlocked cars in Morse code before
We took off running to say living is winning

Lake Shore Drive reads Chicago is 'living
life city' (quoting the song)   winning.

4

The whole street   ladies
lay afloat in the gondola
stroll   of their own legs

the daylit lanterns of their dreams
hide inexpressibly their faces made up
with not being in Kansas

they fan with maps
like feathers of brightly colored directions
to famous brands

of which this street is
that one direction.   And all one direction
only—   no movement.

as if, since people move, there are no people
on this street; the stalks of the buildings, reeds
a hem of the lake sweeps through.

5

daylight you see people's
reflections off each other fill the street
cascading one from another
the crowd slips like a fan out of itself,

in the angling of store displays
the glass facets kaleidoscope a rose
window back
of themselves full of the flash petals of grace

that fall by evening home,
when the ones dressed in evening
wear   possession-less and so, without
reflection here   take all the empties back

all the want and people scavenged back
off the streets   into these who dine with starving   off the streets

6

The street in the opening between buildings
is running a strip of the el like a frame
by frame tape, the windows of the train
different shots of the sky, then it breaks,

and the clouds are caught up in the walls
of nearby glass-skin architecture.
I never get to see what I think
would be the whole movie. I, too, move on.

The turns in the drive roll the buildings
out from behind one another in a scenery
change, only I am the one on wheels,
the drop backs a larger stage than this town.

And just as I can see betrayal coming
by the music, my eyes braille the thunder
hidden even up the sleeve of a silent
film. The hand shakes anyway. Not meant

to be the end of things. An inbound train
toward the loop will be arriving shortly.
The street in the opening

7

The John Hancock Building has never struck
the actual oil it looks like it should.
Wildcatters call this a dry hole. But it isn't,
it has the pool of Lake Michigan

on the bottom when you're looking from the top.
What an amazing hole, he said. Enchantment's name
to call into   what we all are looking for, a spell
to an opening as deep   into seeing.

He had the gift of new   first time in a city,
pick pockets hadn't sighted yet the eyes,
the bulging wealth of openness, the shiny change.
We were watching the old movie of our century.

—our village root, the well's drawn-words drip
into volumes in our pack trying to solve our plot.
A close-up on the winch-rope, frayed
by so continuously raising the question,

cuts off   not to mislead the viewer; and screened
on our bodies, the billboard buses, city wall—
the crude that is this day struck from our drilling

8

All over everything   the sun rises funny.
I heard *the eagle flies on Friday* as
the eagle shits on Friday where I lived.
Not enough for any growth to get paid

its flowers. Mostly weed. Bouquet of distraction.
Broken glass season gives way to plastic
in the lots, only the packaging changes,
it snows something or other year round

white to deal with, powder or rock. Or through
the window, the country unable to stop
opening its poverties, making the sun go 'round
to the back. But the sun reserves its someday

someday to shine where door don' 'llow light.
And I am drenched by a slow, barely brought in
gusher of my working through the cracks,
a gold opened in myself like a vein through

blinding pain, through the names of need and silence.
But my someday come seems didn't
when the hit is only mine, not also enough of to my brothers.

9

Dawn burnished
        wave,   smoothed free of everything
but the slowest curve
                barely less than earth's

hump   unloads
        a surf-less silence
we can see—

                clear bright yet shimmering—stillness as.

Stillness as a dangerous surface   *enough!*
        a floor walked all night
clear to the end of nowhere   got *to get my hands on some*
                no place   except where
                                money from somewhere
                                to get me over this hump
an arm swipes
        everything off the table to
this floor   the hit bottom come to
        the surface   *on the table*

6:03 am.

> The black crown of a sparrow
> a thumb print on
> the air   still wet   morning
> suddenly on file
>
> with the rest of the wanted on
> the old post office wall
> the trellis in wild blossom   birds
> having no jail

FLOCK LIFE

They fly these snap
roller coaster curves,

these taking your breath drops
and lifts   drawing out the stretch

and rebound anyone watching feels
and all without their flying apart—

within unison in   untamable directions
when in a sense they fly in place.

and all other movement emerges out of
keeping out of each other's way:

squalling patterns, the dash, the lilting shapes
just happen out of their correction for

each other's shifts almost as if
forgiveness is to fly.

NOLAN,

The apparition of these faces in the crowd . . .)

riding the bullet train
the view passes by so fast
it is either a blur they say

or —like night lightning
strobes the raindrops
to a stop in midair

in that soundless moment—
maybe from the train you can glimpse
waiting there

one of those famous petals stopped still
in midair holding its wave to you
in place.   write us

and tell us if
this is so.

RELATIVE TIME

Teach in the corner room on the odd# floor
and you are facing down the el tracks a couple blocks

If the train has picked up speed you have to stop
as at a crossing light stop
                              what you're saying
until the noise crosses
                              you can read faces
If it hasn't taken away your train of thought

hitched on in the yards away outside the window
to the track that close you have to grab it

you can get back to business back from your sense
of a head on collision of spaces
                                        the room
passing through the aisle of a train with no more seats
the only reason you don't stay aboard
                                        you catch
the car where you are in the next sentence
back into the train use in images of   relative time.

GAUNTLET

for Kamau Brathwaite

A flatbed of crushed car chassis,
      scrap piled
four or five high holds up
      two lanes of traffic;
the load has shifted
     and curves out over,
the right lane under
     a metal rock-outcropping.

The roadway tier
     has a street just below
the right-hand guard-rail,
      no one below which
is paying an avalanche
     in position
any attention:
    why the truck *can't* change lanes.

Cars in both lanes
     behind the truck hang back
from the crushed which threaten
      to crush us
within the tube of this surf
     of our waste,
to wipe us out.
  You'd think no one'd dare try this gauntlet.

But in the city of the quick
     New York
minute,
    you see the cars on their mark get set

ALL AT ONCE

Trees have whole streets
                         of when they were planted
plaqued with when the city is
                          to inherit them dead
of age almost all at once as if
                         a natural bombing.

People see a bill not figured in,
                          a blood red
collection come
                 like fall's leaf   due without fail
an unseen cost of the design:
                 pale bud and yellow blossom—

though seeming little to do this time
                          with tense spring
in the window
                     of dead and dying trees' terms up,
with expecting a life by life replacement—
                 not this plague of life's time

as a season across the city.
                          By trial we do, but don't
know how death counts the rings
                          from trees to clocks,
species to singled soul
                 at its hour. or on history's days we all die at once.

MACHINERY

Don't start me talkin', I'll tell everything I know.
People up here signifyin', somebody got to go.

The wind will actually rock the parked cars,
spill the nonsense waves of their alarms
back into the surge come off the lake;
crushed chassis, ice jams stack up the chained-
down sound rocking on their flatbed, the shore;
spring's scrap meltdown ahead.
Weather's that kind of big machinery here,
the freakin' schedule is always heavy.
You got statues look like a scrap metal dump
in the park where the yuppies walk their dogs,
you don't know who shoved that shit through.
Someone always under investigation—
And that's the nice stuff. Don't start me talkin'—
the cops killing, the hiring like a family tree

What happened to the city of the big
shoulders? It's still here; it got into power.
Once the shoulders shouldered into power,
power slipped down around the gut and pats
        itself all the time   The wind blows

CENTRIPETAL FORCE

Almost a missing piece
almost invisible the little plane
hauling
      the big summer drink banner
across the offshore sky above the beach crowd
is pulled on hard through its crack-the-whip turn
in this wind.
          The sailboats leaning in unison,
tugged onward by their own silent advertisement.
These are the days to spend.
                And time,
the summer   is pulled out of our pockets
as on its string. Ridiculous clowns piling
out of our midget car of a life.
              The pilot outside
the jokey circles he turns in   needs the money
to keep everything from flying apart,
filling in the missing payment at the center
                    of each turn.

ON THE SPARROW: NO BLAME

When I worked in the steel mill
the ceiling crane dropped a bolt
at my feet   the way the cat
leaves his catch on the doorstep
for me   to step over it
a bolt thick as a sparrow
the gift of it: it didn't
easy as eggshell crack my skull.

Walking underneath the el's
same bridge superstructure
when I first arrived
in Chicago   this is what
I thought of   a falling bolt,
having to give up my cats
and not be mad if the whole
thing falls off track aimed at me.

Buildings straight up from the street
tall slough off their "Falling Ice,"
stand-up sidewalk signs like it's nothing.
Buildings the sparrows slam into,
fall from—   watched from the window desks—
mistaking light for the sky, land up here.
The cats probably have been
put to sleep by age by now. No blame.

SFUMATO

The hummingbird eats what he weighs
every five minutes for twelve hours
if he sleeps and fucks the other twelve;

consider he's eating in
flowers, his head deep in the fragrance
our pheromonal sweat boutiques work up as disguise.

And after his pigging, the hummingbird's breath?
Is he like—as we aren't—honey taking on
the tastes of its source, the smell?

Was eating a banquet of hummingbird eating
jasmine,
a sfumato of living in

brushed out limits of forms?
& where do we put it all?

PLAYGROUND AND PARKS DEPARTMENT MUSIC

The longer all night
the bird-like backup signal
of the snowplow sings,
the deeper I don't have to
guess the snow nest is.

.

I just have to get out,
hatch the morning-shift migration
from its shell   white sleep
with the windshield scraper tooth
that falls through its own crack.

.

Fallen out by spring,
egg-tooth and baby feathers,
then the gulls falling
on scraps, their airbrake squawk
of garbage truck

.

calling. Seasonal
landscape language Spanish
finally the birdsong
of arrivals, guessed words I sing
joining in

.

nesting in lunchtime shade on the grass.
They'll be summer boats, migrating south

down the lake next month. Sky reflects in the puddle;
on the grass, necks raised, geese stage for flight,
wavy lined entry at the border. People
turn a page of the colors.

PART V OF THE EARTH

A LOW BANK OF CLOUD

But for a low bank of cloud,
    clear morning,   empty sky.

The bright band of light beneath the cloud's gray
    I thought at first was open distance,   but it's ice

that by extension raised the lake above the lip of blue lake
    and spilled it farther out than that horizon

along the sky
    and floods the clouds.

    Seeing the distant level further
unfurl into the sky says not to trust

    blue line as terminus
when a meniscus of ice

    can ride up that wall of the skyline,
a measure of illusion how close

    the eye can be to filled
with seeing,   to widen instead the tube of that measure

of sight we are given.   There is the larger
    lake the wider look we open

eyes to see. That glance of the lip
    put in a bigger cylinder falls away,

but how much deeper the spring
    to fill the cup.

As if the surface we are seeing
    drops   the more seeing is added,

    while we feel the stories well as our height
from which to see.   And watch the dawns coming.

. . . I seem to be emptying
of time   the more time I put in,

    and see like a man with weathered eyes enough
to face to face up   to the sight's field expanded

    to insight.   To the dark the lake can turn
and curl up like a map for poems to have

these likenesses to graph,
    then come un-scrolled from semblance back

to just this lake.   Water
    cities are led to   layout

beside.   But never in stillness;
    always the restoration to change,

from ice, from cloud, turning to clear
    liquid—as is most of our body

    water—   thinned sheet, layer
that if written   on or with,   a bearing

a name chiseled on water
    disappears.

WATCHING FOR THE ANCESTORS

A stop here to sit
has made an imprint of

my butt
the waves wipe

the sand out from under   nestling
a seat

firm as a mother's
hand beneath her baby

beneath me   waking me
out

of a dream
of the floating. I

slap my own cries off—
like they were sand

—standing up,
as a wave fills this hollow.

OF THE EARTH

to Luis J. Rodriguez

Angel of pelicans, the huge sack
that brings the drowned back unswallowed
coughed to their feet   stretches
thin as water;   and
as the newborn's natal skin
that sloughs off   it is the water
drying.

The 'sleep pull their wake shirts off over their heads
and drop the inside-out body
of their clothes here   on the floor's beach.
I believe you when you say, Luis,
water is the skin of the earth.
The pull thinnest of that water, the air,
carries in its sack inside-out   our lungs.

Angel of the frigate bird, of the puff fish,
the huge earthen word that emptying out
is world for us,
I believe you when you say
water is the skin of the earth.
Carried in the skin of the earth, the black
blood of The Crossing carries me.

SONG TO ANUBIS

who followed us like a dog
here

    A few
bony dog clouds
of sand   sniff around the tent
as if picking over
      it like garbage

    Or the desert
shifting around for a place
to lie down   to settle through
its counted moment
      addressed through

    the neck of an hourglass
The slag
teepee of timing   *coyote, knock*
A few ingots of hot cloud
      stars to-be

    spinning around
Up above my head   *Anubis/* coyote,
knock the ash from your pipe at this door,
There must be a
      folding away

    of all this moving around
that will not be a packed
to go hole in the ground,
but be the filled internal wound
      healed and gone

ROAD IKON

Vacant black square
   windshield eye
      shades,
the glistening muzzle teeth
   of the tractor-
      grill,
the fuming mirage
   of asphalt breath, burning
      earth it lifts over:
Road monster   meso-
   american in
      its mask's iconography

Or should be   a Tula stone
   temple summit,
      from a view that on ascent
up those stairs, appears
   to dawn rising over
      the termination in the sky
of those steps   the horizon
   of the pyramid top
      but instead—
here   the tops of these hills
   these mountains   have the wings
      of two exhaust clouds,

have the eon thunder as
   their eighteen gears,
      the mask of coming weather here—
a truck rising over the hill . . .
   Who doubted the force of that collision
      with these spirits
doubted that it could throw your centuries
   aside
      into your face   into its heart

Land

Spirit of
The place   the nature
gods

RUN

Ice   moon   in a pot;
Dawn warms chilled valleys.   Fog makes
A last batch   of night.

                                              ice   : moon in a bowl.
                              dawn stirs chill valleys   fog takes
                                            last helping of night

Coffees of rest stops;
Spring pours.   Streams warmer than air
raise early spirits.

Road down night mountain
First light   hits the valley's floor.
Flash in driver's eyes.

                                        guard rail   length missing
                              first light   hits the valley floor
                                    night driver   wakes up

Guard rail length.   Missing
turf   re-laid somewhere below;
Hollow   grace fills in.

My hand on the wheel;
That spot where tire touches road.
Turn held here so brief.

                                        rain feet   dancing with
                              windshield wipers side to side
                                        each step clears the last.

Horizon,   silo;
Changes in size are minutes
Horny   home to you.

THE HEAVENS

We can't see over the curve,
    so horizons

front for the whole beyond,
    lessening limit

with their non-existence
    as literal

point for point beauty
    for what isn't seen.

Or,   beyond's gate exists
    only seen not to reach;

when in fact,
    waves approaching from our wake's forward

through its line
    wash back

the line's other side to us;
    that once *nowhere*   throwing on a crested robe at turned up,

beyond
    —as if still damp from a shower—

pulling on a fog in the mirror
    for us to write our I see yous through,

to slip ourselves between the folds   be pleased
    to consummate arrival's terms for paradise

come round,   horizon's expectations
    for climax

to its mirage—
    wrapt around the sphere:

all those Heavens
    fronting for the plain unfound.

THE ORIGINAL DEED

Scrolling darkness blurs the letter of the stars
to luck   to illegible text except
for one direction struck across the page;

the dotted line across the bottom sky,
a distant highway   whose signature is ours,
is human   more claim than covenant.

The first we'd ever really seen
The Milky Way, Dick woke us from the sleeping bags
all nervous, "Something's different." "Dick," we said,

"the earth turns and we look out at different
stars from the different places. We ride, it
moves   past and over us."   We went back to sleep.

Dick saw the Native come to see our sleeping
just as he woke; we all found scorpions
warming under us when we packed up,

though none of us was stung.   That highway we saw
last night was the one we had tried for
a shortcut to   across the desert on these bikes.

The failed attempts of creation
are going to run across themselves
or some self not themselves and not quite recognize

themselves and not quite realize
they've come across success, come across the last step
which may be ghosts of them.

CHORUS

During this dawn, the bronze trees
re-create creation's mistakes
leading to green   leaves.
The small wooden crowd of humans,
their new tentative flesh   concludes
the celebration by moving
along   going their ways
having days.

The trial dew fails away at the sun.
The golds, early   buy into that clear
in the spectral air.   The colors cash in their
delineations   for things   for keeping with
a roulette eye that lands on the rainbow,
cash in and layout the world like drinks

all around!

*

All Creations have worked down to this one.
The histories and character of them all
at one with variety   Its safety
in the possibilities   Their loss hedged
in retained pattern within pattern emerged
if not inchoate   deeply apt.

And maybe   the exact luck-up that's needed
and we'll know   not to try that trick again.
In our bones.   The salmon swim
in perpendiculars of the water
fall   skate up the avalanches   fly —

Maybe what should be hallowed is the mistake
that sends the endlessly repeatable
unit   off-shape into shapes the fuck-ups try.

*

All things are possible but not all
possibly successful
The *eureka* heard as likely as *oh shit*
I'm sorry I'm sorry   no one to hear.
One of the loose ends that this time leads nowhere
is half of   in our hands   what wires us here.

In a vast scale of catastrophe and loss,
systems of order create themselves,
self-organize a higher simplicity
it's said. This said   for our reason   our ecstasy.
But say it doesn't apply to me singular?
Order so many numbers of star higher

it hasn't got here.   And won't count
off   remaining off in my time.

TRIBAL TAG

The peppery smell of eucalyptus burning
in the jungle says you're coming up on people
like sweat says people   or pee does   the specie
name in this info clear in the smell   as in
the subway tunnels of New York or its alleys,
startles you with its welcome reassurance
after days away from civilization   home
if only to a different peoples' woven huts
the surprised stare and wave between strangers
and the clear   identifier of asking
for water and it given   then in return
the shared strip from a piece of sugar cane to say
we drink/ eat—   a graffiti pretty much the same
as our faces say so—   we are you don't kill us

                            .

Bodies and actions spray and paint the moment
of contact   passing in our hand on who it is
who is playing and in what body's borders
what street of the old story we are on
tagged with this latest label of appearance
here   the information of our making
these adornments of touch or run woven
to determine if this flesh is worn or eaten
between us.
                    We offer rice from our supplies
They   the spitted and fermented corn chicha
communal drink and a roasted insect cone
of larvae   the delicacy we respect with our picking
these to eat one by one from the cells
                                The rice bagged
in one of our socks he carries off between his legs—
                a penis the house opens to laughter

BOY GOD QUETZALCOATL WATER SHAPE STOOD

1.

(the potty training)

I dreamt I was jade, and the boy I was
in the pajamas, lit a secret glow-
in-the-dark ring green from inside.
I was dragging a stone statue by the arm
a toy that also glowed but with my history's
I will see you later light   in the dark.
I was standing in the dark
looking into a brightly lit room

The adults of light sit at a sea
of a table   playing some game
and they were laughing.

Now here I am
on the side of a road in Mexico
waking from a dream of water in a tub
standing up out of itself
in the shape of a boy.   A claw-foot tub
in a bathroom that is the
whole peeked into
sky from the dark of a long hall

from the long haul to wake
from the back of a van realizing
I have to pee   And the boy,

aquamarine crystal Quetzalcoatl,
the kid, waiting in the Museum of
Anthropology in Mexico City,
but there   in rose alabaster
naked, his legs slightly bent,
and he's laughing   or as if gotten up
in the middle of the night
of trans-dimensional life   and he has to pee.

And as he watches from there
me pissing here   I realize
I am pissing on peyote.

2.

(the water stood)

!   Look up from sleep
at the road open out ahead from the back
of the van sleep   from the floor of the van,

from sleep ahead   between their backs
shadows of the heads of the driver and
the passenger   as a frame to look through,
see how the road's heat reflects the sky
making it water I can see into,

a shadow-framed windshield   as if in through
a door open   look into a bright bath
room   in on an old
claw-foot tub out of what memory
of water   water dazzled
at its own blinding transparency

water standing up in the shape of that child
shape
of that wonder of having to pee I could see
right through   Quetzalcoatl
the boy god shaped water of
having to pee stood up out of the water

I must have said something Then
when we pulled over   when we walked off
into the desert wakened
by the young Quetzalcoal just outside
Tula on the way to Mexico City
there he is he wants me to water his peyote.

I know   when I see god I'll remember
we can laugh about having these little kid erections
for a reason.
The clean separation of a spirit from its medium.

3.

(the architectural orders of plain sight)

This pole cactus   stack
from a wind cleared area around it

in an already nearly swept empty
desert   the almost structure

the piling hand still on it
hidden as the house in it   that it is.

all the building   the piling together
seem accidental nothing to notice in

the settled ends of drift become a lean-to
we discover someone occupies.

he's disguised the natural debris
into a room we can see   where he sits

in shapes on the ground inside brushed away
by no other dust devil, witch's whirl

than stays here   than hides the husbandry
these are   ordered rows of peyote.

Lined up in a piss stop a walk from the truck
our shadows fall across the lines

on the ground written through our streams of
water we notice we're kids peeing on peyote.

LAST OF THE BUSH BATHS

(an ethnopoetic)

A cold fog almost a steam
bath's thickness
sits on the salt   towel of the beach streets
not saying anything,
which is to say no traffic.

Chicago's not asleep,
just not up
to it. The sight of the lake
has not gone off somewhere,
but it's there   but it's Sunday.

An all-nighter is its own alarm:
the frozen surface waves
in the mirror   bent out of shape, discordant;
he needs to soak loose the hunted's
instinctive freeze in place   loose,

at least backed off enough to free a cold sweat
and give this shit a rest . . .
This steam room isn't the good pipe and healing
song from years back   when
we tried to re-imagine the sweat lodge

from somebody else's story into our own
arms' welcome . . . This salt is trucked.
This is for sobering up.
after the long search parties in
whiteout hallucination.

AS A TOOL OF THE LANDSCAPE . . .

As a tool of the landscape, the ocean
rules off a line of purest horizon
as base to the sky.
         The earth rests,
a graphed page in a booklet of tests
we only know we haven't studied for
                and with our crossing
out of line   of thought
we cannot pass.
Beyond his own backyard, no one remembers

much of the larger garden. We are weeds.
Rather than its tool or wielder that we were,
maybe it's good to be leveled with
as the growing, not the eternals,   among the grownups

---

staying in school the life
of the learned interpretations
the beautiful   may simply be
delay   a way to go
first class   deluxe to darkness

with school   in the end
you have to get out   in the end
and get the job in the ditch
of nothing   in the end
the end

FEAST OF THE MISSING

Sea is always tossing back a wreath
    of its water up the beach.

Fish markets raise from their spread tables
    the smell body

of blessing from the dead
    cooked;   no one sees fragrance

as the roll away of what was stone.
    Any give and take

tide of the eat and the eaten thanks
    to propitiate

any imbalance, any gluttony
    that would privilege

death over life to keep
    just   itself alive

has to float on a wheel of returning
    self   unrecognizable

that comes the direction   no one looks
    until he catches   on

IMPONDERABLE THIRST

As if we are always asleep,
the jaguar's tracks are there in the morning,

they lead from the forest up to the gathering
of the unreal leaf-work of our lean-to,

lead up to our exhausted bodies already
in the bags asleep.

As if we are always asleep
the end comes

right up to us and stares into our sleeping eyes,
ignores us and continues on its way.

The tracks seem to gather around us
in the steps of some consideration,

then go around behind and down to the river,
and back into the forest—

which we wake and look towards
and see nothing.

PSALM *(a line-singing of)*

The psalm goes
The Lord is my shepherd
          fancy French-made insulated climbing boots
          and almost   we cannot walk where shepherds do

          because our boots cannot get past each other
          in the rut   over ten thousand feet up

          that countless Andean feet have cut
          their foot wide   and half up a shinbone deep,
I shall not want
          and out of which I shall not want me
          (camel-like backpack of my acquired and all)
easier for a camel to get through
          to fall, to be unthreaded   as it would be to be thrown
          by a trip up of myself
the eye of a needle than for a rich man
          and make the hell fall   as geological
          as the thousand feet down the canyon wall
beside still waters
          to where fallen I would land
          beside rivers in same paths so far below

          they are not heard   *still.*
          the treacherous movement also then   called still.

FLIGHT RECORD

One night, flying cross country, I look down
the sides of the Sears and the John Hancock
Building towers, looking down the walls,
a well of electric water, the drawn lights
lift along the structures occulting the shadow
outlines of the verticals, the parallax
making deeper the dimensions of depth.

Some cities look like the embers of a fire
when you fly in. Against the faint points
of the glowing ash, what might have been
the scale of flames you don't want to think about.

And once, coming in late down the Hudson
into Newark, I could look up Forty Second
the whole way across Manhattan like peeking
through a crack into more light than light
across the universe, by the convergences
a worm hole off to the side on night's horizon.

Or come into Quito during the day,
you make a long gently rocking sidle up
against the ridge on one side, on
Pichincha's slope down, and you
still above those clouds climbing its meadows,
the sharp fall away to the plateau and its
distant other volcanoes
                              then the ground
suddenly rises up to meet you as
and on a ledge with its whole city on
a shelf   and you land. That's it.

The transition from the ground seen by air
to my feet on the ground, the change
from my winged like Bird to like birds putting
their wings behind their backs to strut away
as if on the earth is on the money like this

I accept
the spaced wells of the cities sounded out,
or, in the glass, my shadow portrait on the lights,
even the most darkly changing window
remembered view

from the crash flipping over taking off on water,
settling right side up enough to hang
me from my seat belt then set down
where we could swim ashore,

or from the cabin door, the: "Step
off the plane . . ." into a field deployed
overgrown with aimed escort, the cocked rifles'
uniforms   plumaged in rounds of ammunition
seeming to arm the trees around that landing
strip in the jungle—   I accept the change.

I accept the change
from thin air, empty handed for all I've seen,
from air to the walk away again in all my flesh,
accept what I have to leave
of flight for feet.

The wild geese that floated to the ground
down their river of air dip their heads
into the grass, though the black bubbles
of their necks suggest a surface risen,
a froth from their landing, swallowing them.
Like them, nothing seems clean anymore.
Whether the sicknesses of cash or the earth
dying, green shit all over everything.
Too many geese, too many people live
in too many places unsuited for
the body of their gross activity;
and the idea of making place like home
takes the clothes off someplace else, like logging
takes the wood and kills the root that held another place
in place.

It's clear in that photograph from space
there is only so much place on the earth
for us, no place else to go, the rest *is* space:
that difference, a limit stark as life
-and-death was before this shot's perspective.
The sight, a sci-fi alien view, but true;
and true there's never been any invader
who wasn't we whose traits *we* made alien
in what we've done somewhere to ourselves.
A screen full of ships from 'cross oceans of space
come to take us slaves, their bug-eyed profit
jones, their multiple arms for gimmee, their color—
in our mirrors. The flash flood of a life form
from elsewhere in the human universe, is us,
we land.

The innocently plaintive song of geese
is all about us even as we taxi their runway
chalked on our walk among them through the park.
So large mannered have our movements grown
that all the earth is as if too short a runway
for each step, for geese who stay their migration

where we keep the cut of grasses packaged
the most convenient for them, for wild
coyotes in Chicago who walk into
McDonalds fast, shock the counter, get food.
We can't say why we don't call this a robbery,
it's so city slick for an animal,
we see the folktales have their basis after all.
The disingenuously plaintive songs of geese
pass it on.

The song is "Needmore have harm a many man."
where having nothing wears a proper name
even though its line admits, "I need a shirt/
to get up out the dirt"   to put something on
its name. Coyote re-invents his world by breaking
and entering rules: coyote rules! Read the headlines.
We think that all the crows do is make noise
because a shadow is not evidence
even cast through light on film,
but something clearly says, "Move over."
Nothing new, we've said it to ourselves.
How do we not   and break our own rule,
reset the how much of things   how who is one?
One person, one species, one world to know
enough.

The blues knows weather and clothes have to fit,
and that fit is a place a highway keys open for it.
But when the roads themselves flap like the tarps
over the few goods those fleeing can cart
on them, destination come loose from an end—
what would enough be wearing in this weather?
If, like the sage, we find him in the road,
where could enough carry a clean change?
Or do we meet enough as no more,
as resigned among the exhausted, finished
and finishing any fill of every cup
with smashing things up.
. . . or in the ruts of the fleeing,
do furrows appear?

THE BIRD THAT WALKS ON LILY PADS

It looks like he lifts
long strands of dripping algae
with a stick
                    when the bird that walks
on lily pads lifts his feet   the fan of twigs
the structure on the rafts he makes of leaves
to walk on water
                        at the aviary.

I carry laundry   on a stick
from the kettle at the camp
that way
                    or spaghetti from the pot

to the plate equivalent of lily pads floating
on the picnic table mats   if there aren't any
of those kinds of birds
                            on the river

I can fill in for that
geometry.   And when my brother finally talked
after coming back
                        from the fighting, he had seen

a head on a stick from both armies; it was a while
before we could do things we use to together
like even grill steaks.
                            I would have waited longer

on his explanation for that
But now we talk   go to the aviary, fishing, the zoo.
Sit drawing in the dirt with sticks—
                            And talk.

*

The area around the aviary
in the park insists on meeting you
as the inside of the building with its sound
walking up to you to escort you through
the door gently nothing but bodiless calls
of birds beside you in that way you can't see.

Inside, you can't see them immediately,
you see their rooms of elegant foliage,
staged water, and light in movement before you see
them moving the leaves leaving one for another;
the room waves as if their wings brought up the wind
moving, or you've entered a room already dancing.

One of the rooms has a quiet not from silence
but of a sound so low you can't tell how long
it goes on as if waiting is part of it,
but you can't see where the long breathed or bowed
note is coming from inside or out again calling in,
it makes you take a seat while you wait to place it.

They fly free around you, so it could even be
just that feeling of escort as you entered
just behind you or one call of them all that surrounds you,
such a far away song so close the leaves
on the plant beside your bench move   the far away song
steps around the planter, the bird had been there all along

with me.   I'd seen nothing fly up to where I sat,
the song came sparingly and barely audible then
I was telling you about my brother finally talking
about it long after he'd come back from the war.

EARTHENWARE

Through the window, the orange of the streetlights
dries out the shadow wetted white walls,
the desiccated orange and chalk of red crockery
I sleep inside, a hazy moon ball of spider.

This room upturns itself open to night
dropped   dream seed of soaring blossoms winged
lifting the winter sky in their beaks.
An aged pot agape like the beaks of nestlings.

This resting mostly not the beautiful we wish
restored, still cracked
all the shed we have to brush out
the earth   pot   clean

soil and turn
another spring make ready on the wheel.

AS AT THE FAR EDGE OF CIRCLING

As at the far edge of circling the country,
facing suddenly the other ocean,
the boundless edge of what I had wanted
to know, I stepped
      into my answers' shadow ocean,

the tightening curl of the corners
of outdated old paperbacks,   breakers,
a crumble surf of tiny dry triangles around
      my ankles sinking in my stand

taken   that the horizon written
by the spin of my compass is   that this is
is not enough   a point to turn around on,

      is like a skin   that falls short of edge
as a rug,   that covers a no longer
natural spot, no longer existent
to live on from,   the map of my person
      come to the end of,   but not done.

      That country crossed was what I could imagine,
and that little spit of answer is the shadow—
not the ocean which casts it—   that I step next
into   to be cleansed of question.

      But not of seeking   . . . it as
if simplified for the seeking,
      come to its end at this body.

A SLIM VOLUME TAKEN INTO THE PROVINCES

I have to leave early in the dark
and hungry to avoid
crossing the snow as the noon

burns the crust
into an un-servable lake
slush instead of the crisp bridge

that would be in order
to get me over the ridge

My journal is already laundered clean
of my words   and my instructions
have dissolved

into a white mash   a washed bone
ball   rolled into itself
of all I have in the world   in my pocket

The ink is thin the paper is poor
my eyes balance on the pale
words around which a stream

flows   almost erasing
the way across
the idea

Shadows   the black flowers
of the light self
-sowing through the trees

dark gardens   of midnight
for the gray-white morning
hour   of blindness

in print miles before I am
to arrive   here

To approach the waiting milestone
dims whatever else of its lantern
'til only the placed light there is on me.

In this light   barely   but used to it
I can make out the staggered columns of my account
as if back through weren't the real distance:

the thin chest flag pinned on by each ridge
the titled introduction taking your coat each storm.

My letters and ribbons have been the natural—
strengths on their way to the more—
natural weaknesses—   and loss.   yet—

I wonder where I thought I was going—
to 've done what you must pass
examinations for before I took any.

EMPTY SKY

The day's change emptied
from my pockets: copper pennies

on the desk surface,   pads
their water lily figure graphs

as wet   the shiny newness.
The pond star not yet

risen above
the daily furniture of horizon,

the desk polished to water
I see just the thought of flower beneath.

     The coins cast   the buy the gamble the act
of   faith in the offering

pennies   the luminous bread on
the blotter   a felt green pond

water   emptied of the changes
the mind's been through

today   returns
a stillness.   Bursts upward

not so much the flower
not smell—   a radiant sting further up
     between the eyes   from behind the ears
     from up the back of the neck
the days changes emptied

     Pocket out of   which is
emptied the take

on flesh as sack
of bones of walking craps winnings   the day,

jackpot in
the body as container,

entire nirvana lake of coin
figures   of blossom   bells and whistles

empties as it fulfills.
This shirt off my back

     nakedness
puts me in the street

the dewy job or no
job to undress from   works or none

done.
I've lost everything

to those pennies'
wakening of the surface on a desk

only permanent
as moving water or the changing

     light I draft   thirst for.
     The bowl of my
day   turned up   held out
and the larger sky

clear
emptied into it

ABOUT THE AUTHOR

Ed Roberson is the author of *When Thy King Is a Boy* (1970), *Etai-eken* (1975), *Lucid Interval as Integral Music* (1984), *Voices Cast Out to Talk Us In* (1995, winner of the Iowa Poetry Prize), *Just in Word of Navigational Change: New and Selected Work* (1998), *Atmosphere Conditions* (2000, National Poetry Series winner), and *City Eclogue* (2006). He has received the Lila Wallace–Readers Digest Writer's Award, and was a finalist for the Lenore Marshall Award from the Academy of American Poets in 2000. In 2008 he received the Shelley Memorial Award from the Poetry Society of America. Born and raised in Pittsburgh, Pennsylvania, Roberson has worked as a limnologist (conducting research on inland and coastal fresh water systems in Alaska's Aleutian Islands and in Bermuda), as a diver for the Pittsburgh Aquazoo, in an advertising graphics agency, and in the Pittsburgh steel mills. As twice team member of the Explorer's Club of Pittsburgh South American Expeditions, he has climbed mountains in the Peruvian and Ecuadorian Andes and explored the upper Amazon jungle. He has taught at Columbia College Chicago, the University of Chicago, and currently teaches at Northwestern University.